Pandas Live Here

By IRMENGARDE EBERLE

Doubleday & Company, Inc., Garden City, New York

PICTURE CREDITS

American Museum of Natural History, p. 16, 21
China Photo Service (from Sovfoto), p. 26, 31
Eastfoto, p. 57
Robert C. Hermes from National Audubon Society, p. 22
Gordon Smith from National Audubon Society, p. 11, 14, 52, 60
Smithsonian Institution, p. 6, 12, 19, 54
United Press International, p. 25, 35, 37
Wide World Photos, p. 32, 38, 41, 42, 44, 47, 48, 51, 59

Other books by Irmengarde Eberle

BEARS LIVE HERE
BEAVERS LIVE HERE
A CHIPMUNK LIVES HERE
ELEPHANTS LIVE HERE
FOXES LIVE HERE
KOALAS LIVE HERE
MOOSE LIVE HERE
MUSTANG ON THE PRAIRIE
NIGHT ROVERS

ISBN 0-385-01719-7 Trade
0-385-04465-8 Prebound
Library of Congress Catalog Card Number

Frontispiece — Hsing Hsing in the Washington Zoo

Pandas Live Here

In the wild, in their natural home, the big black and white pandas live in rugged mountain jungles. There are but a few of them in all the world, and they live only in a small area of the Far East—largely in the Szechuan province of western China, in Tibet, and in Nepal, north of India.

Off and on in the last thirty years or so, a few pandas were caught by men and sent to zoos. Wherever they were shown, crowds gathered to look at them. Panda charm touches everyone.

There is a puzzle and quite a little mystery about the handsome and likable pandas. For thousands of years they have lived in about the same regions, yet in all that time most of the people, even those quite nearby, seldom if ever saw one. No stories or legends seem to have grown up around them. And only one artist, in the seventh century A.D., is known to have made a picture of one.

Part of the mystery about them, then, is that they were known only vaguely for so long. For giant pandas, as they are called, are quite big—about five feet, or a little over, from snout to tail. And they are striking-looking. Their fluffy fur is marked in great smooth areas of black and white, and they have round black tufts for ears on their white heads and black rings around their eyes. Oddly, a panda has a sixth finger on each front paw, growing out of the wristbone.

Though records show that as early as 2205 B.C. a few Chinese knew pandas existed, it is clear that the animals did not arouse interest among either the scholars or the general public then or for centuries afterward. Probably they were seen by too few, and too rarely.

Not until an Englishman in the Indian service saw one in the snowy mountains at the border of Nepal did anyone in the Western world know of them. Actual interest began to pick up much later when a French missionary and nature collector in the Szechuan province of China heard of them. In 1869 he asked a native hunter, who had seen one, to shoot a giant panda and bring it to him. In this way the missionary got the skin and not only sent it to the French Natural History Society in Paris, but wrote a letter describing how the animal looked before skinning and everything he had seen and heard about this unusual and little-known creature.

After that, other missionaries and one or two adventurous European hunting men came to China and looked for the new kind of animal—but only rarely with success. The few who did shoot any brought back only the furry hide—not a living panda. That, they thought, was not only too difficult, but almost impossible.

The animals were very hard to find. There seemed to be too few of them, the native hunters reported, and they were very secretive. Their dark and white fur looked like splashes of sunlight and shadow in the jungle, so it was easy to miss them. For a long time the pandas were left pretty much alone.

But gradually the European and Asiatic naturalists became more interested. They not only asked the native hunters for skins, but also for

the whole skeletons of pandas. When they received them they artfully rebuilt the animals from the skin and bones, mounted them, and showed them in museums. Those that were so preserved in recent times are of course far more perfected than the early ones. The accompanying photograph of a panda diorama made by today's experts and set up in the American Museum of Natural History in New York, is a wonderful example. It also shows something more — the beauty of the mountain region where these animals live.

In the early days of the giant panda discovery, the hunters and scientists found another animal new to them. It was only about two feet long, and its tail was as long as its body. It also had quite differently marked and colored fur from that of the big pandas. In fact, to you or me, the lesser panda looks like an entirely different kind of animal. But the two have some characteristics in common. To scientists both seem related to raccoons and also to bears. The final decision as to just which group these animals belong to is still to be made.

This book is only about the giant panda—as cuddly-looking as a very big teddy bear. However, pandas are not always gentle, and they have unusually strong, hard-biting teeth. To be really tamed they have to be caught at a fairly early age and brought up in captivity with affectionate care, as the world's few zoo pandas are today. Even then they sometimes become moody as they grow older. And they can be dangerous.

In the wild, natural state, pandas live on rugged mountains, 5,000 to 14,000 feet high. The slopes around them are covered with thick forests of fir, oak, and bamboo. So dense are the bamboo jungles, that hunters often cannot see more than a few feet—perhaps five or ten—ahead of themselves. Roving mists make the high wilderness still more secret-looking. All of this is fine for wild pandas hiding from men. But it also adds to the mystery clinging to them.

That bamboo grows so far up in the mountains at all is something of an oddity of nature. Bamboo, really a tall grass though it looks more like a tree, is a plant of the plains and of warm or hot tropical climates. Somehow this bamboo, which grows only about twelve feet tall, has come to thrive at very high altitudes, in thin air, in places where there is often snow a large part of the year. If it were not for the bamboo the pandas would not be there, for bamboo of this particular kind is their main food.

In the spring and summer they eat only the luscious young green sprouts and fresh leaves. They also feed on some other plants, such as certain vines, bunch grass, and irises. Of these latter they eat roots, bulbs, flowers, and all.

In winter most of the plants dry up and shed their leaves, and there are no tender sprouts of bamboo. Then the pandas eat the coarser, harder branches and twigs. As this plant has almost iron-hard stems, those strong teeth of theirs are a necessity. They bite the hard branches off the main stems, crack them open and eat the inside, then drop the leftover woody part. They swallow many big, hard splinters too, but the walls of their digestive systems are very strong and tough, and so the splinters do not harm them.

Sometimes in the winter, wild pandas have a hard time finding enough food. Some naturalists think that they may eat a few small animals then, such as rodents and birds, and perhaps larvae too. But this is not fully known. Even if experiments are made while a panda is in captivity, that does not necessarily mean that pandas would eat the same things in the wild. And not many observations can be made at first hand in the thick mountain forests and jungles.

Actually the bamboo belts are so dense in places that the pandas have made tunnels through them to move about in. That is, their frequent comings and goings, and their nibblings in certain places, wore out the branches in time, and so the passages were formed. These are often too low for men to travel in. So even the pandas' tunnels remain partially secret.

In the worst of winter many of the pandas that have been living in the higher mountains, perhaps at the 14,000-foot level, come down to 7,000 or 5,000 feet. There the snow is not quite so heavy, or so unbroken month

after month. The food problem is partially solved for them too because when they cannot find enough to eat on top of the lighter drifts, or on the bare earth, they can dig and perhaps find those bulbs of the wild iris and the roots of a few other plants that are to their taste.

In spring pandas are on the upward move again. Many may go to the areas where they were the year before. It is almost always very cool so high in the mountains—even in summer.

The pandas spend much of their time eating. Often they sleep wherever they are, when they feel the need for it. However, in cold weather they are apt to find themselves a shallow cave, or a hollow in a great tree, and make themselves a nest of bamboo twigs and leaves.

They do not hibernate as some animals do. In warm weather and even in autumn, they often fall asleep out on the forest floor or draped over a rock. In zoos they have been seen asleep lying on their stomachs with their four legs spread out.

That they were largely unknown to most people for such long ages is one mystery about these animals. That we don't know what animal family they belong to, or much about their life in the wilderness, means more mystery for us. And why there are so few of them—that's another. Most animals increase in goodly numbers over the centuries. Especially is this so when animals are not hunted by men, as pandas weren't for long ages. Besides, adult pandas probably have no animal enemies either—except leopards. But pandas caught by hunters do not show scratches or scars which would be signs of fights with the big cat animals. So leopard attacks may not occur often. It seems pandas may be accepted among them and most other wilderness creatures as animals to be left alone, because of the fearful power of their bite, and their strong, sharp claws. So the adults are fairly safe.

However, sometimes the mother pandas leave their very small young in a hollow tree or cave while they go to nibble leaves and stems quite far off. Then wild dogs, bears, or leopards might be able to trace these babies by their cries and scent. They no doubt make a good meal, and that might play a part in keeping the panda numbers down.

Again the harsh climate may kill some of the very young ones in their first weeks, but we do not know this.

Adult pandas are loners. Twice a year there is a mating season, one in spring and probably one in autumn. Then both males and females look for mates. A male begins to sniff for the scent of a female on bushes, tree trunks, and grass. And somewhere else in the jungle the female sniffs to find *him*. Sometimes one will stand on its head to leave the scent from a musk gland near its tail. In a zoo, pandas do this against a wall, fence, or even while on a swing. In spite of this scent placing, it is quite likely that a few may not find mates in the thick jungle. After all, there are so few, and they are often scattered far apart. So non-mating, too, may account for some of the scarcity of pandas. After they mate, adult pandas soon part. Each goes his own way to eat, wander about, and rest as it suits him.

The female pandas, who find mates, have their babies six months later in or about April and August, depending on when they were mated. Usually the parents have only one cub, perhaps occasionally two. The mothers care for their young almost constantly. They hold them in their arms; sometimes, as seen in one zoo, they pat them gently, cuddle them, and play with them almost as human mothers do.

The western edge of China's Szechuan province is almost all mountains. These lie east of the still higher Himalayas. In early days, probably before the birth of Christ, as we measure time, Chinese peasants settled on the scant and small plains in the valleys between the high mountains. They planted rice, millet, and some other foods that would grow there. As the population doubled, tripled, and then increased still more, there was not room for even the tiny farms of all the growing families. So some went up into the mountains and settled wherever there was a little flat land between the crags and rocky outcroppings. Some of their farm patches were only five or six feet wide. They could not plant rice there for lack of water. But every foot of usable land was planted with some kind of grain on which they depended for food. (In recent years that included American corn too.)

These early people and their descendants probably never saw a person from the Western countries until one or two Europeans and then Americans came there because of their interest in pandas. The pandas were in the high reaches of the mountains and largely kept out of sight. The ranges, and especially the peaks of these mountains, are famous for their beauty. To the native people they were often mysterious-looking, especially when they were partly hidden by the mists. The peasants began to think of them as divine.

As for the pandas living up there in the bamboo and fir forests, they were even more deeply hidden than the peaks. Most of the villagers had no opportunity to see them at all. A few have said they thought a panda had occasionally come down to their hives to steal honey. But pandas are so secretive that this seems unlikely. The honey-stealers were probably bears.

Some of the native hunters climbed far up the crags, and these men, in time, saw one or two of the pandas. They called them *bei-shung*, which means white bear, and they considered them divine, too, as divine as the mysterious mist-hung mountain peaks.

Over the ages some of these hunters must have shot a panda once in a while—long before white men urged them to. They were probably not aware what the animal was. They skinned the pandas they had killed, along with those of bears. All of them used hides, but mostly those from real bears, as sleeping mats. A very few panda skins have been found by Western searchers in some of the makeshift huts of the native hunters, and one or two have been found in homes of the people in the tiny mountain villages. Yet almost all these people said they had never seen one of the animals. Fortunately a panda's fur is not as soft as it looks. Down the middle of the back, over the spine area, the hair is coarse and makes a rather stiff ridge. So panda hides are not very comfortable to sleep on. This fact may have saved more pandas from being hunted and killed by the natives over the ages.

In the nineteenth and early twentieth centuries, as the interest in pandas spread in the outside world, a new danger for pandas arose. Museum directors of several great cities began to ask for pelts and skeletons to study and exhibit. Then native hunters, mostly in China, some in nearby mountain countries, began to hunt pandas for Europeans. The regions where the animals lived were so difficult to reach that not many succeeded. This, too, was a blessing for the pandas. But when the Natural History Museum of Paris, and later museums of a very few other cities of Europe and America, began to show mounted pandas, which they had reconstructed from the skins and bones, still other museums wanted like ones.

The first American white men to make an organized expedition to China's Szechuan province to shoot a panda were Kermit and Theodore

Roosevelt. Sons of Theodore Roosevelt, who had been President of the United States in the early nineteen hundreds, they undertook the mission for the Field Museum of Chicago in 1929–30.

Most of the great and ancient civilization of China has always been concentrated in the eastern part of that vast land. There lies Peking, and there the big seaports are to be found. Szechuan province reaches far into the interior of Asia, and the mountains where the men hoped to find pandas were on the borderline between China and Tibet. Tibet at that time was a separate country. Western Szechuan was a sparsely settled region because good farmland was so scarce there. It had few roads and some trails which had been used since ancient times in a little trade with distant cities.

The Roosevelt brothers arrived in China, and taking a Chinese naturalist with them, made their way to the far western part of the country. Then they set out in earnest for the hunt.

Reaching the mysterious, shrouded mountains, they rode upward over rough trails. Once in a while they saw a shrine or small, plain temple. Again they were in untrodden wilderness. But for many days and weeks they found no pandas. They saw other creatures though. The bhurel, the wild blue sheep of the region, especially impressed them, as did the small musk deer. On the advice of natives, the Roosevelts went northward. About a hundred miles farther on, they came upon some native hunters who said they had recently seen a panda, a bei-shung, somewhere in the surrounding wilderness. With new enthusiasm the brothers now

began their search again, skirting the dense bamboo jungle at one place, but able to enter it at other points.

At last one day they saw a panda! It was lying asleep on the ground, and they were able to shoot it easily. The coolies brought the dead animal down the mountain slopes for them.

The Roosevelts' panda skin and bones were taken back to the United States and to the Field Museum in Chicago. There they were mounted to look like a live panda and placed on view.

The attempts at shooting a few more pandas for such purposes went on for quite a while. Luckily only a very few hunters succeeded.

But more and more Americans, and people abroad, wanted such panda displays as the Field Museum then had. And more did get them. The Free Natural History Museum in Philadelphia, for example, got a group for mounting in 1931 — the skins and bones of two adult pandas and a small young one. The United States National Museum in Washington got fifteen such sets of the remains of pandas between 1929 and 1942. Some came from Tibet and Nepal, but most came from the Szechuan province of China. The hunting and shooting went on, and the few pandas of the world became so much fewer year by year.

Next, museum directors and other naturalists decided that they must have some live pandas for their zoos. That way they could study them further, and the public would be able to see these attractive animals as they really were. Now men from several countries talked of setting out on this kind of mission.

In America, in 1936, Ruth Harkness, a dress designer, said she would capture one alive for an American zoo. Her husband had wanted to try for one but had died before he could fulfill his wish. Mrs. Harkness laid her plans carefully, and she asked a Chinese naturalist to join her expedition.

It was a very difficult journey, and it was unusual, in those days, for a woman to cross the whole of China from an east coast port to its far western edge. It was still more difficult to climb and search in the high, rough, forested mountains.

Among those peaks, in the small villages, she engaged some hillmen who knew the region. She and her party then searched for weeks. She had almost given up hope of finding a panda to trap when, one day, one of her people heard a whimpering sound that seemed to come from a nearby hollow tree. He called Mrs. Harkness' attention to it, and she hurried to look into the hollow. There before her lay a very small baby panda. It was obviously only a week or two old and was about six inches long. It weighed only about two pounds, and its eyes were still closed.

She took it out of its hiding place and with her party began to make her way down the mountain. Beyond the high bamboo belt they came to a very small village again. Here she bought milk for the little panda. Then she and her party hurried on.

The lady petted and bottle-fed the baby panda and took as good care of it as she would have of a human child. So they came out of the mountains and onto the foothills and plains, and then started the journey back

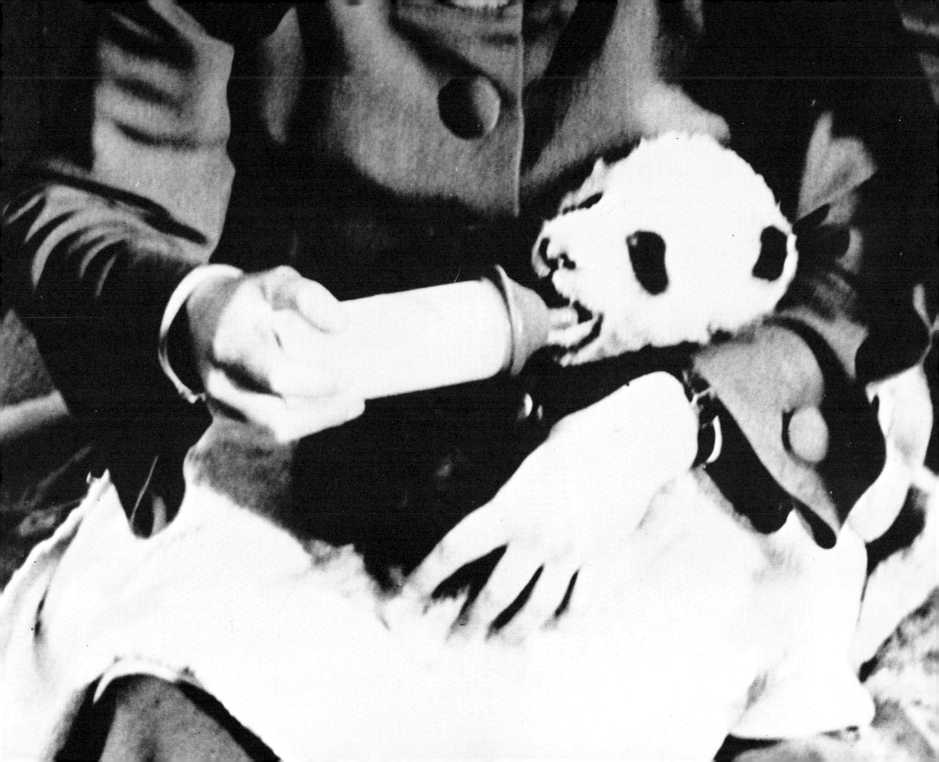

to a port city on the faraway east coast of China. There she boarded a ship and sailed for America.

Landing in the United States a few weeks later, Mrs. Harkness came eastward and showed the baby panda at Chicago and New York.

He had grown rapidly in the two months or so of his life and now weighed thirty-six pounds, but he was still quite small and very much a baby. He was affectionate and trusting with Mrs. Harkness.

Eventually she took him to the zoo of the Chicago Zoological Society at Brookfield, Illinois. She chose that zoo because she thought the organization there was best fitted to take care of Su-Lin.

Mrs. Harkness had named him Su-Lin, meaning, in Chinese, a "little bit of something precious," and that he certainly was.

He lived very contentedly in his new home, quickly getting affectionate with his keeper. As to food, he soon was given cereal with his milk and later the fresh bamboo leaves and stems he then needed. The zoo sent for these periodically. He remained very tame and seemed to be well and thriving. But in about the middle of his second year he died.

The naturalists at Brookfield Zoo had learned a good deal about pandas from being with him daily during his short life. They wrote reports and articles about him so that other zookeepers and directors could share in this knowledge.

The interest in pandas, stimulated by Su-Lin's charm and his unusual

qualities as a rare animal, made other zoos want live pandas more than ever — both for study and for the public to enjoy.

A few hunters of Europe and America, and natives of Szechuan province in China, now began to search for pandas to take away from their mountain homes alive. The Page expedition was one of these. The photograph shows one of the Pages carrying a young panda in his arm after a trip by airplane. These and other men learned how to trap them without hurting them. A very few brought out one or two of the heavy animals from their bamboo jungles one way or another. Some of the natives of Szechuan brought their trapped ones down in large, oval, basketlike carrying cages. Most of those caught were not full grown, but some may already have been one hundred to two hundred pounds in weight.

The carrying baskets made the task easier for the natives. Trying to catch young ones instead of fully adult ones was a good idea too. The pandas then were of course less heavy than the fully adult three-hundred-pounders — and therefore less of a strain on arms and backs. There was another advantage in catching fairly young ones, for these adapted themselves to their new life in zoos more easily than the adults would. Most of the youngish ones came to be devoted to their keepers in the zoos and seemed unafraid of the strangers who gathered in swarms to look at them. But almost all of the zoo pandas became less good tempered as they grew older.

The zoos of the world that had live pandas, after the Harkness panda was brought to America, were: the New York Zoo in the Bronx, the St. Louis Zoo in Missouri, and Chicago's Brookfield Zoo—the last named had several after Su-Lin died.

In other lands they were in the London Zoo, and the zoos of Moscow, and China. The Chinese had the largest number of them, especially in recent years. This is natural since pandas are native to their land. They have made a special effort to study them and to improve their handling of the pandas in their zoo.

The zookeepers wanted live pandas despite the fact that not many of the animals that were captured lived long. Many died on their way to a Chinese port, or on a ship sailing for Europe or America. Naturalists and animal lovers everywhere began to fear that in a short time these rare and charming animals might become extinct. And there was real danger of that.

The United States turned down a young panda in the late 1950s because it was from a communist country. Its name was Chi-Chi. England took it, and it lived to the good old age of fifteen years. Eventually the Chinese passed a law preventing pandas in their land from being hunted for hides or taken out alive. At last the wonderful pandas were somewhat protected.

In the United States a panda in Chicago died in 1953, and the one in New York in 1957. Then for many years there was none in all America. But there remained a longing for them.

The cities with zoos which still had pandas, when China clamped down on their export, were London and Moscow. They decided to try to mate theirs—since England had a female and Moscow a male. They hoped that in this way they would begin to learn how to breed pandas in zoos, so that they would not become extinct and so that more people of the world could enjoy them.

So England sent her Chi-Chi to Moscow on a visit to the male panda there. But things didn't work out as the naturalists had hoped. Chi-Chi would have nothing to do with the Moscow panda. She ran from him and sometimes crouched, watching him as if to make sure he would not come close to her. Once she hit at him with her paw.

Finally the keepers separated them. The experiment was given up and Chi-Chi was sent back to England. There, it is told, she showed great joy at seeing her keeper. It was clear that in the years of her zoo life she had become a people's panda instead of a panda's panda, as she had been when still in the high mountains of western China.

The zookeepers everywhere had learned a good deal more about pandas' habits and needs in the years while they still had them. They exchanged information with each other through notes and letters, reports and articles in natural history publications. Some of this information had to do with food. They had found that besides their favorite bamboo, pandas will eat such things as apples, carrots, certain green vegetables, cereal, toasted honeybread, green cornstalks, and the leaves of the soybean plant. They will sometimes even eat a little meat, though they are certainly basically vegetarian now. Much of the bamboo that our first few pandas ate was grown in Florida, and a fresh supply was flown to the zoos as needed.

Since they chew much of the time, they will sometimes pick up a dry bamboo stick for that purpose when there isn't any fresh young bamboo handy. This frequent chewing keeps their jaws and teeth strong.

Another thing zoo directors and keepers all agreed on is that when pandas are quite young they quickly become affectionate and are as friendly as they look. But they studied further the fact that pandas often become moody and even a little grouchy when they grow older. They were careful not to touch these animals carelessly, for they might bite with those extremely dangerous teeth of theirs. One zookeeper had his hand bitten off by a full-grown panda. But it was decided that such moods, such acts, can perhaps be accounted for: zookeepers are very affectionate with the pandas when they are young, but have to give most of that up when the animals become adult and strong. Perhaps the pandas then miss the petting and so develop bad tempers. Or the truth simply may be that it is natural for them to become that way in maturity.

Again, pandas are not usually friendly with other animals, but one is known to have become pals with a Persian ass in an adjoining cage-pen. He went to the wire fence often to sniff at him and apparently communicate with him.

Playful young pandas are a delight. They sometimes do all sorts of things that look as though they were putting on an act to amuse the human audience. One panda puts its empty food pan on its head. Another waves the pan or gives it a last fond lick. One stands and looks as though he wanted his portrait taken. One lies on some logs, its head supported by a front leg. Sometimes one will lie on its back and play with straw or a branch.

Usually if a zoo has two or more pandas the animals are kept in separate cages most of the time, because they are basically loners. But often they are put together in the same pen for a little while, and then they usually play with each other. They chase each other, put their snouts together, eat from pans standing side by side. But they don't object when they are separated again.

Pandas sit up more than they stand. But they walk on all fours, pigeon-toed like bears. To eat they bring the food up to their mouths with their front paws. They do not put their heads down to eat like dogs, horses, foxes, and so on. Sometimes, it seems, they sit up for the purpose of making a yipping or barking sound. They clean themselves often, comb-

ing their fur with their claws. But they don't lick their bodies except when they have spilled food on themselves. They are probably not great swimmers and bathers. But they will sit in water when the weather is hot.

Zookeepers once bathed a panda in a tub of soapy water. It was a young and well-petted one. They would not have risked it with an older one, because then it is just about certain that they would have been seriously bitten.

Ling Ling in the Washington Zoo

In China—the pandas' homeland—the keepers and directors have been trying to breed them in captivity, as the English and Russians tried. Finally, a few years ago, the Chinese succeeded—two baby pandas were born in the Peking zoo about a year apart. This is quite a triumph.

In the spring of 1972, after President Nixon's visit to China, the Chinese government sent us a fine gift—the two young giant pandas that are now in the United States National Zoo in Washington. As almost everyone knows by now, the female is the older and is named Ling Ling. The male's name is Hsing Hsing which is pronounced Shing Shing. They are charming the thousands of people who have come to see them in their carefully prepared compounds. There they have air conditioning to make the air more like that of the cool mountain slopes of China. It's not only pleasant for them but keeps them healthy.

Their carefully planned diets are based on previous experiences of zookeepers who had pandas under their care. The two animals are housed next to each other so that they can be loners when they prefer, or greet each other with sniff and paw at their partition.

In the coming years we will learn still more about pandas and their jungle homes in the East. In time some of the secrecy and mystery about them may be largely gone. But they will surely always delight and amuse us with the things they do and the way they look.

Irmengarde Eberle has written over sixty books for children, and some of them have been published overseas in twenty-seven languages.

She came east from her native Texas shortly after graduation from college to become an editor and a writer of adult articles and fiction. Her keenest interest lies in writing fiction and factual books for the young, particularly in the warm portrayal of animals to children as accurate natural history. She collects the illustrations for her wild-animal books from the outstanding wildlife photographers of the United States and sometimes of other countries. She has won several awards, and a number of her books were Junior Literary Guild selections. Five universities have asked to collect her manuscripts and other papers. The main collection is at the University of Oregon.

She served at one time as a reviewer for the New York *Herald Tribune's* book section. She was also one of the originators of the Children's Books Section of the Authors' Guild and for ten years their Children's Book Committee chairman. She has lectured at Columbia University's writers' workshop and elsewhere.

She and her husband, Arnold W. Koehler, live in New York City.

DATE DUE

APR 12 2011	
APR 12 2011	
OCT 23 2012	

GAYLORD   PRINTED IN U.S.A.